THE HISTORY OF THE MOTION PICTURE

BY BARBARA A. SOMERVILL

◀ 1891
Thomas Edison
develops a
kinetoscope.

◀ 1420
Magic lanterns are
used for the first
time.

▲ 1997
Titanic costs
$400 million
to make and
market.

A.D. 1000   1200   1400   1600   1800   2000

Content Adviser: John W. Hiller, Former Curator of Photographic Mechanisms, Smithsonian Institution, Washington, D.C.

THE CHILD'S WORLD® • CHANHASSEN, MINNESOTA

Published in the United States of America by The Child's World®
PO Box 326 • Chanhassen, MN 55317-0326 • 800-599-READ • www.childsworld.com

ACKNOWLEDGMENTS
The Child's World®: Mary Berendes, Publishing Director

Editorial Directions, Inc.: E. Russell Primm, Editorial Director; Katie Marsico, Managing Editor and Line Editor; Judith Shiffer, Assistant Editor; Rory Mabin and Caroline Wood, Editorial Assistants; Susan Hindman, Copy Editor; Jennifer Martin, Proofreader; Judith Frisbee, Peter Garnham, Olivia Nellums, Chris Simms, and Stephen Carl Wender, Fact Checkers; Tim Griffin/IndexServ, Indexer; Cian Loughlin O'Day, Photo Researcher; Linda S. Koutris, Photo Selector

The Design Lab: Kathleen Petelinsek, Design and Art Production

PHOTOS
Cover / frontispiece: left—Bettmann/Corbis; center—Hulton-Deutsch Collection/Corbis; Donald Pennington/Corbis Sygma.

Interior: 5—Randy Faris/Corbis; 7—HIP/Art Resource, NY; 8—Christel Gerstenberg/Corbis; 9, 14—Archivo Icono-grafico, S.A./Corbis; 12—Hulton|Archive/Getty Images; 13, 17—Bettmann/Corbis; 16—Blue Lantern Studio/Corbis; 19—Gary Hershorn/Reuters/Corbis; 22—Warner Bros./The Kobal Collection/Picture Desk; 24—Universal/The Kobal Collection/Picture Desk; 25—Murray Close/Corbis Sygma; 26—Getty Images; 28—Lucasfilm/20th Century Fox/The Kobal Collection/Picture Desk.

LIBRARY OF CONGRESS CATALOGING-IN-PUBLICATION DATA
Somervill, Barbara A.
  The history of the motion picture / by Barbara A. Somervill.
     p. cm. — (Our Changing World—The Timeline Library)
  Includes index.
  ISBN 1-59296-440-0 (library bound : alk. paper)
  1. Motion pictures—History—Juvenile literature. I. Title. II. Series.
  PN1993.5.A1S573 2006
  791.43'09—dc22   2005024785

TABLE OF CONTENTS

MAKE A WISH!

Nana's birthday was two weeks away, and Katya wanted to give her something special. For a week, she taped her family with the camcorder. She caught Mom in the garden swatting at a bee. Dad lay snoring in the recliner. Alex whacked a home run at Little League. Cara pounded out Mozart on the piano.

Katya transferred her pictures onto the computer. She added **digital** photos of Nana and Granddad. On the Internet, she found a film clip of a birthday cake with blazing candles. Using the computer's moviemaking program, she put together a film. Katya was **producer,** director, scriptwriter, **cinematographer, narrator,** and editor of *Make a Wish.*

At her birthday dinner, Nana received a book from Alex and a picture frame from Cara. She thanked Mom and Dad for a blue sweater.

After dinner, Katya and her family sat down in front of the TV. Katya pressed the remote and showed Nana her gift. The opening credits rolled . . .

Computers play an important role in modern moviemaking.

MAKE A WISH

A Katya Production

In association with Katya Films

Starring Katya Litsova (And her family)

A smile spread across Nana's face. The family applauded, and Katya dreamed of one day winning an Academy Award.

CHAPTER ONE

SHADOWS ON THE WALL

Several thousand years ago, a fire burned brightly in a dark cave. Shadows stretched and danced against the cave wall. Perhaps this was when humans first became fascinated by light and motion.

Shadows have entertained people from many cultures. Centuries ago, Chinese, Greek, and Javan artists created shadow puppet shows. Java's Wayang Kulit Shadow Theater dates back to A.D. 900. Puppets on rods moved between a light source—fire or candles—and a screen. Audiences watched as shadow puppets told tales of good and evil.

1400s: MAGIC LANTERNS AND PEEP SHOWS

By 1420, magic lanterns changed mysterious shadows into real pictures. Magic lanterns were simple slide projectors. A projector is a machine that uses a screen

The Wayang Kulit Shadow Theater opens in Java.

A.D. 900

Vikings sail the Mediterranean Sea.

to display images or movies. The magic lantern's slides were painted sheets of glass. Light passed through the glass and projected, or cast, pictures on a cloth screen or wall.

In about 1437, magic lanterns led to the invention of the peep show. Peep shows worked much like modern **kaleidoscopes.** Viewers looked into one end of a wooden tube or box. When they pointed the other end toward a light source, a scene appeared. Peep shows did not become really popular until the 1600s.

1646: THE GREAT ART OF LIGHT AND SHADOW

A German priest named Athanasius Kircher became fascinated with the effects of light and shadow. He experimented with

Magic lanterns (right) are used for the first time.

1420

Europe is in the midst of the Renaissance.

the magic lantern and the *camera obscura,* or "dark room."

People had been using the camera obscura since the 1500s. A scene or figure outside a box was transferred through glass lenses onto a flat surface. Artists used the camera obscura to trace pictures on canvas before they painted. In 1646, Kircher experimented with lenses to project clearer images into the box.

Some historians incorrectly believe that Kircher created the magic lantern. Kircher improved the device, but he did not invent it. He discovered that magic lanterns needed adjustable lenses for better focus. Kircher simply introduced a new and improved version of the 200-year-old magic lantern. His model was capable of better projections. In

Athanasius Kircher experiments with the camera obscura and magic lanterns (left).

1646

Sir Thomas Browne is the first to use the word *electricity.*

1659, Dutch scientist Christiaan Huygens developed the magic lantern that was eventually used in most theaters.

1799: *PHANTASMAGORIA*

In 1799, Belgian Etienne Robertson used the magic lantern to introduce the French to a new idea in entertainment—pure horror. Robertson's *Phantasmagoria* had everything today's movies offer, including light, sound, and special effects. Since it was a slide show, the only thing it was missing was true motion.

The theater fell dark. Thunder rumbled. Lightning flashed. Skeletons, demons, ghouls, and goblins danced through the air. Women fainted in fear. Grown men hid their eyes. People could not wait to buy their tickets!

The French line up for tickets to Etienne Robertson's *Phantasmagoria*.

1799

The Rosetta Stone (right) is discovered in Egypt.

Throughout the 1800s, similar shows drew large audiences. Families gathered in churches or halls to view lantern shows about Christmas, fairy tales, or Halloween horrors such as *Phantasmagoria*.

The next step toward motion pictures was three-dimensional (3-D) views. This allowed people to see an image's height, width, and length. Such pictures had depth and did not simply appear flat on a screen. In 1838, Sir Charles Wheatstone **patented** a **stereopticon** that let people see in 3-D. But Wheatstone's stereopticon was bulky and difficult to use. In 1849, Scotland's David Brewster developed an improved model that provided many evenings of entertainment.

1838

The stereopticon is patented.

John Deere develops a steel-tipped plow that allows settlers to till prairie soil.

CHAPTER TWO

FLICKERS

Two photographers—Eadweard Muybridge and Dr. E. J. Marey—gave the invention of motion pictures a boost. In 1872, wealthy Californian Leland Stanford hired Muybridge to take pictures of a galloping horse. Stanford wanted to know if a horse's four hooves were all off the ground at any single moment. It took Muybridge until 1878 to complete the project.

Muybridge set cameras along a racetrack. He attached strings to the cameras and stretched them across the track. Then, a racehorse named Abe Edgington galloped through the strings. As the horse broke the strings, cameras snapped pictures. Muybridge proved that a running horse does have all four feet off the ground at once.

Using photography to show motion fascinated Muybridge. Unfortunately,

Eadweard Muybridge photographs a horse galloping.

1878

England's William S. Gilbert and Arthur Sullivan produce *H. M. S. Pinafore*.

his technique required many cameras. That's where Dr. E. J. Marey entered the picture.

Marey invented a photo gun that took several pictures in a row. By 1888, Marey's photo gun could snap more than 100 shots in rapid order. He projected the photos quickly by turning a crank—and motion pictures were born.

Inventors scurried to develop cameras and projectors that improved on Marey's photo gun. In the United States, inventor William K. L. Dickson began work on a projector called the kinetoscope. Dickson worked in Thomas Edison's lab. Edison was famous for several inventions, including the lightbulb. It took several years to develop the kinetoscope. Although the work

Dr. E. J. Marey's photo gun (left) can snap more than 100 shots in rapid order.

1888

National Geographic Magazine is first published.

done in Edison's lab proved important to motion pictures, the first true moviemakers were Auguste and Louis Lumiére.

1891: EDISON'S KINETOSCOPE

Thomas Edison looked at Muybridge's work and saw the possibility of moving pictures. Although Edison did not invent the kinetoscope, he held patents on inventions that were developed in his laboratory.

Edison believed that the future of motion pictures was in single-person viewing. His 1891 kinetoscope was a one-person viewing booth. A projector showed films that ran about fifteen seconds. Unfortunately, Edison did not offer his kinetoscope to the public until 1896. The Lumiére brothers of France beat him by one year with their first

Thomas Edison develops a kinetoscope (right).

1891

James Naismith invents basketball.

13

motion picture presentation.

1895: THE LUMIÉRE BROTHERS

The Lumiére brothers presented their first motion picture to an audience in the Grand Café in Paris, France, on December 28, 1895. They called their camera and projector a *cinématographe*. Their invention was based on the work of Dickson and Frenchman Charle-Emile Reynaud. People paid to see their movies, which the Lumiéres created with amazing speed.

Lumiére productions were simple and short. Within two years, the Lumiére catalog offered 358 films. These films often featured everyday scenes such as women washing laundry, men leaving a factory, or families eating dinner.

Auguste and Louis Lumiére use a cinématographe (left) to present their first motion picture to an audience in Paris.

1895

X rays are discovered by German physicist Wilhelm C. Roentgen.

CHAPTER THREE

FROM SILENTS TO TALKIES

In 1905, Harry Davis and John Harris opened a motion picture theater in Pittsburgh, Pennsylvania. Shows cost a nickel. Audience members stood—the theater had no chairs—but shows lasted only fifteen to twenty minutes. The first film shown was *The Great Train Robbery.* Davis called the theater Nickelodeon, combining the cost (a nickle) with *odeon,* the Greek word for "theater."

For five cents, audiences watched one or two silent movies. Music and sound effects came from a piano or organ beside the screen. Crowds kept coming . . . and coming . . . and coming. Soon, Davis and Harris opened a 96-seat theater and served 7,000 customers daily. Their Nickelodeon was a hit!

Within two years, the United States had about 5,000 nickel theaters. Some

Harry Davis and John Harris
open the Nickelodeon.

1905

Norway declares independence
from Swedish rule.

had seating, some didn't. But people flocked to nickel theaters even if there wasn't a place to sit down. After all, radio and television didn't exist yet.

1911: *LITTLE NEMO* TAKES A BOW

Almost immediately, cartoonists saw a chance to bring their work to life. In 1911, Winsor McCay developed several **animation** techniques to change his newspaper comic strips into animated movies. Early cartoons had a coarse, jerky appearance. Every **cel** was hand drawn. McCay's first animated movie, *Little Nemo*, featured 4,000 separate cels.

The journey from comic strip to stardom was a

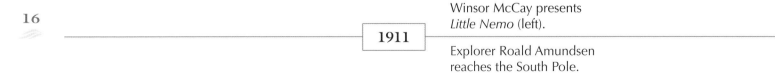

1911

Winsor McCay presents
Little Nemo (left).

Explorer Roald Amundsen
reaches the South Pole.

short one for the first animated superstar—Felix the Cat. Drawn by Otto Messmer, Felix made his movie debut in 1919. Felix got into one fix after another and kept audiences laughing for years.

The world's best-known cartoonist and animator was Walt Disney, creator of Mickey Mouse. From 1923 to 1927, Disney drew a motion picture series called Newman's Laugh-O-Grams. Disney's first cartoon star was Oswald the Lucky Rabbit. Oswald starred in *Trolley Troubles* in 1927. Mickey, Minnie, and the gang came later.

1927: A BIG YEAR AT THE MOVIES

Cartoon characters made audiences smile, but human actors made them cringe, weep, shudder, and laugh. Adventure,

> "IT IS AT THE MOVIES THAT THE ONLY ABSOLUTELY MODERN MYSTERY IS CELEBRATED."
> —ANDRÉ BRETON, AUTHOR

Felix the Cat becomes the first cartoon superstar.

1919

Airmail service (right) begins between Chicago, Illinois, and New York.

horror, romance, and comedy lit up the silent silver screen.

In the 1920s, movie tickets cost between fifteen and twenty-five cents. Audiences watched cartoons, news, and feature films. Organists provided music, train whistles, drum rolls, and other sound effects. To follow the story, viewers read captions that appeared on the screen.

As movies became even more popular, studios such as Warner Brothers, Fox, and Paramount went into full production. They released movies with amazing speed. They didn't worry about music because they made "silents." Movies cost little to make, and—even at a quarter a ticket—profits were good. Silent stars such as Mary Pickford, Charlie Chaplin, Douglas Fairbanks, and

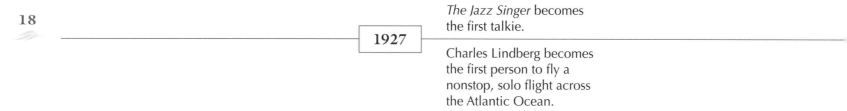

1927

The Jazz Singer becomes the first talkie.

Charles Lindberg becomes the first person to fly a nonstop, solo flight across the Atlantic Ocean.

Rudolph Valentino packed theaters across the country.

In 1927, a major event changed motion pictures forever. Silents became "talkies." Warner Brothers produced *The Jazz Singer*, starring Al Jolson. As the movie opened, audiences heard Jolson say, "Wait a minute! Wait a minute! You ain't heard nothing yet!" And that was the truth.

The Jazz Singer steadily sold out. Other studios soon began making talkies. Fox Studios produced the newsreel Movietone News. Newsreels were short films that focused on current events. Weekly newsreels became an alternative to reading newspapers. During the first full year of talking movies, audience numbers rose by 30 percent. Talkies were here to stay.

> "THE TALKING MOTION PICTURE WILL NOT [REPLACE] THE REGULAR SILENT MOTION PICTURE."
> —THOMAS EDISON, 1913

1928

Academy Awards (right) are given out for the first time.

Alexander Fleming discovers penicillin.

CHAPTER FOUR

LIGHTS, CAMERA, ACTION!

Black-and-white movies were entertaining, but real life came in color. Studios experimented with producing color films. They shot film through green and red filters. They glued two strips of colored film together. They dyed film. But realistic color did not come until a company called Technicolor developed its three-color process. This process required three layers of film—red, blue, and green. When light passed through the joined strips, realistic color was projected.

In 1932, Walt Disney's studio produced the cartoon *Flowers and Trees*. This was Disney's first venture into three-color Technicolor. *The Three Little Pigs* followed, and audiences responded with enthusiasm.

By 1934, Radio-Keith-Orpheum (RKO) studios offered its first live-action,

Disney wows audiences with a full-color cartoon.

1932

The United States struggles through the Great Depression.

full-color release—*La Cucaracha*. A year later, *Becky Sharp* became Technicolor's first three-color feature-length film. (A feature-length film is the main show at movie theaters. At that time, most theaters also showed short newsreels and cartoons.)

During the next few years, several movies made the jump into color: *Gone with the Wind*, *The Wizard of Oz*, and Disney's *Snow White*. But color did not bring about as many changes in movies as sound did. A dozen years after *La Cucaracha*, nine out of ten movies were still black and white.

1950s: CINERAMA SCI-FI

The 1950s began a period of big-screen viewing, musicals, and cheap science fiction. *This Is Cinerama* opened at

DRIVE-IN MOVIES
IN JUNE 1933, RICHARD HOLLINGSHEAD OPENED THE FIRST DRIVE-IN MOVIE THEATER NEAR CAMDEN, NEW JERSEY. DRIVE-INS BECAME THE RAGE. MOM AND DAD PACKED DRINKS IN THE COOLER. KIDS WEARING PAJAMAS SETTLED INTO THE BACK SEAT. FOR A LOW PRICE, THE FAMILY CAR TURNED INTO A PERSONAL MOVIE THEATER.

1935

Becky Sharp is the first three-color feature-length movie.

Construction is completed on the Hoover Dam.

the Broadway Theater in New York City in 1952. The film required three projectors, an extra-wide screen, and seven sound tracks. (Sound tracks are the narrow strips on movie film that contain sound recordings.) The Cinerama system resulted in films that were large in size, but that were also too expensive to continue making.

During the 1950s, science fiction burst onto the silver screen. In 1953, *The War of the Worlds* showed audiences an alien invasion of Earth. A year later, *Creature from the Black Lagoon* dripped out of a swamp. And in *The Blob,* an oozing mound of what looked like

1952

Broadway offers wide-screen Cinerama (left).

Jonas Salk develops a vaccine to prevent polio.

raspberry jam terrorized a small town. Hollywood offered ninety minutes of fear for about fifty cents a ticket.

Science-fiction monsters came to life through single-cell animation. Animators posed miniature models of horrifying creatures. They took a shot, moved the monster, and took another shot. When the shots ran together, the monsters appeared to move.

1974: *EARTHQUAKE* AND SENSURROUND

During the 1960s, movie sound went from piano tunes to musical scores played by famous orchestras. A score is music that is specifically written for a film or theater production. But even though movie sound had come far, sound technology still needed to advance.

3 - D

PUT ON THOSE BLUE-AND-RED CARDBOARD GLASSES! IT'S 1952, AND WE'RE WATCHING *BWANA DEVIL* IN FABULOUS 3-D. THE GLASSES ARE DESIGNED TO MAKE FLAT IMAGES APPEAR THREE-DIMENSIONAL. IN-YOUR-FACE 3-D HORROR FILMS AND WESTERNS COST BIG BUCKS. IN THE END, THE 3-D FAD OF THE 1950S DIED A QUICK DEATH.

The science-fiction feature *Creature from the Black Lagoon* appears in theaters.

1954

The U.S. Supreme Court rules against segregation in schools.

An Event...

EARTHQUAKE

Starring
CHARLTON HESTON
AVA GARDNER · GEORGE KENNEDY
LORNE GREENE · GENEVIEVE BUJOLD · RICHARD ROUNDTREE
Co-starring MARJOE GORTNER · BARRY SULLIVAN · LLOYD NOLAN · VICTORIA PRINCIPAL
Written by GEORGE FOX and MARIO PUZO Music by JOHN WILLIAMS Produced and Directed by MARK ROBSON
Executive Producer JENNINGS LANG · A MARK ROBSON-FILMAKERS GROUP PRODUCTION A UNIVERSAL PICTURE · TECHNICOLOR® PANAVISION®

Moving into the 1970s, sound took on new dimensions. The 1974 disaster flick, *Earthquake,* introduced Sensurround. This sound system was so powerful that audiences felt the theater shake during the quake on-screen. Dolby sound followed close behind and provided improved stereo sound.

In 1982, *Return of the Jedi* introduced THX sound systems by George Lucas and Tomlinson Holman. THX offered custom-designed systems for theaters. It worked with individual theater companies to provide sound systems based on each one's specific needs. Today, stereo sound systems exist in most local theaters.

Sensurround shakes audiences watching *Earthquake* (left).

Girls are allowed to play on Little League baseball teams.

1974

1993: COMPUTER-GENERATED DINOSAURS

The greatest change in movies came with computers. Producers no longer hire 5,000 actors for a battle scene. Instead, they hire 100 computer technicians to create images of soldiers. Computer-generated armies move, fight, bleed, and die just like real people. At least it seems that way to the audience.

Computers bring fantasy to life. In 1993, computers created *Jurassic Park*'s many dinosaurs. The beasts prowled, stalked, and hunted much like scientists think dinosaurs did millions of years ago.

Computers create *Jurassic Park*'s (right) dinosaurs.

1993

Bill Clinton is sworn in as the 42nd president of the United States.

Consider how computers have changed animation. Computers create feature-length cartoons that are extremely realistic. Characters such as Mike and Sully in *Monsters, Inc.* move smoothly. Their movements are very different from the jerky motion of cartoon characters from the early 1900s. The backgrounds in modern cartoons appear natural and realistic. Just check out the jellyfish in *Finding Nemo.*

Computers provide amazing special effects that were impossible only a few years ago. Technicians generate crowded stadiums, fascinating characters, and unknown worlds. Computers will undoubtedly continue to allow movies to advance.

Toy Story (left) becomes the first totally digital feature-length film.

1995

The Million Man March is held in Washington, D.C.

CHAPTER FIVE

MOVIES TODAY AND TOMORROW

Today, movies appear on television, in theaters, and directly on video. The drive-in movie has become the "driving" movie, as automobile companies add DVD options to vehicles. New technology brings stereo sound, large-screen presentation, and in-theater atmosphere to at-home viewing. All that's needed is the popcorn!

But modern moviemaking can prove expensive. Take a look at *Titanic,* the top moneymaking movie of all time. When it came out in 1997, *Titanic* cost about $200 million to make. What cost so much? Clearly the director could not build a new ship. Technicians built sets for specific rooms, such as the main dining room or a character's bedroom. Other parts of the movie were

1997	*Titanic* costs $200 million to make.
	Dolly the sheep becomes the first mammal ever cloned from an adult cell.

generated with computers. Editors used new computer technology to put the parts together.

Editing films used to be a cut-and-paste process. Editing was linear, meaning pieces of actual film were cut, placed in order, and then glued together. Today, movie editing is digital, nonlinear, and flexible. Using movie-editing software, the editor can choose sections of digitally-stored scenes and arrange them in any order. Special effects can be created, or several layers of film can be "glued together" to form one scene. Music, sound effects, and voices can then easily be added.

2004: THE GLOBAL MOTION PICTURE

Moviemaking is not limited to Hollywood. Moviemaking

Star Wars Episode II: Attack of the Clones (left) is the first big-budget film shot entirely on digital video.

2002

World Cup soccer becomes television's most watched sport.

opportunities exist in every nation. Portable **generators** and handheld cameras make moviemaking a global affair. No location is too remote for filming. Digital movie cameras allow "instant" views of actors' work.

Motion pictures have changed a great deal since Thomas Edison cranked out his early technology. Movies have gone from black-and-white to color, from silent to sound.

Expect one more big change. Theaters may soon begin showing e-films. Instead of getting a hold-in-your-hand version of a new release, local theaters will receive e-films over the Internet. Luckily, popcorn will still be available in the lobby.

BLUE SCREEN TECHNOLOGY How does Harry Potter's head float in the air? How do normal-sized actors become hobbit-sized on screen? In all these cases, the actors are shot against a blue screen. The blue background is later removed on a computer. Then a new background is added. The actor who plays Harry Potter wears a blue-screen suit. Editors can also make the suit disappear on the computer, so it appears that Harry's head is floating in the air!

Sky Captain and the World of Tomorrow is the first feature-length film combining completely computer-generated backgrounds and live actors.

2004

Massive, peaceful protests in the Ukraine lead to a new and fair presidential election.

animation (an-i-MAY-shuhn)
Animation is the act of turning a series of drawings into a motion picture. In 1911, Winsor McCay developed several animation techniques to change his newspaper comic strips into animated movies.

cel (SEL)
A cel is an individual picture or slide used in animation. In early cartoons, every cel was hand drawn.

cinematographer (sin-uh-muh-TOG-ruh-fur)
A cinematographer is a person who shoots the film for a motion picture. Director Ron Howard is also the cinematographer for some of his films.

digital (DIJ-uh-tuhl)
Digital electronics use numbers to record images or text so that they can later be accessed on a computer. Katya added digital pictures to her movie.

generators (JEN-uh-ray-turz)
Generators create electricity by turning a magnet inside a piece of wire. Portable generators have helped make moviemaking a global affair.

kaleidoscopes (kuh-LYE-duh-skopes)
Kaleidoscopes are tubes that use light, mirrors, and bits of colored glass to produce colorful patterns. Peep shows worked much like modern kaleidoscopes.

narrator (NA-rate-tur)
A narrator tells a story. Some movies include a narrator who speaks throughout the film.

patented (PAT-uhnt-uhd)
A patented invention has received government protection against theft or duplication. Sir Charles Wheatstone patented a stereopticon in 1838.

producer (pruh-DOOSS-ur)
A producer creates a movie, hires actors, and puts up the money to make the movie. David O. Selznick was the producer for *Gone with the Wind*.

stereopticon (steh-ree-OP-tih-kahn)
A stereopticon is a device that gives viewers the impression of a realistic 3-D picture. During Victorian times, an evening's entertainment included looking at slides through a stereopticon.

FOR FURTHER INFORMATION

AT THE LIBRARY

Nonfiction

Hamilton, Jake. *Special Effects.* New York: DK Publishing, 1998.

Hasday, Judy L. *Extraordinary People in the Movies.* New York: Children's Press, 2003.

O'Brien, Lisa. *Lights, Camera, Action!: Making Movies and TV from the Inside Out.* Toronto: Maple Tree Press, 1998.

* Parkinson, David. *The Young Oxford Book of the Movies.* New York: Oxford University Press, 1995.

* Wiese, Jim. *Movie Science: Forty Mind-Expanding, Reality-Bending, Starstruck Activities for Kids.* New York: John Wiley & Sons, 2001.

Fiction

Daniels, Lucy, and Shelagh McNicholas. *Puppies in the Pantry.* Hauppauge, N.Y.: Barron's Educational Series, 1996.

* Books marked with a star are challenge reading material for those reading above grade level.

ON THE WEB

Visit our home page for lots of links about motion pictures:
http://www.childsworld.com/links
Note to Parents, Teachers, and Librarians:
We routinely check our Web links to make sure they're safe, active sites—so encourage your readers to check them out!

PLACES TO VISIT OR CONTACT

Debbie Reynold's Hollywood Motion Picture Museum
One Island Drive
Pigeon Forge, TN 37963
865/429-6425

Universal Studios
100 Universal City Plaza
Universal City, CA 91608
800/864-8372

ABOUT THE AUTHOR

Barbara Somervill is the author of many books for children. She loves learning and sees every writing project as a chance to learn new information or gain a new understanding. Ms. Somervill grew up in New York State, but has also lived in Toronto, Canada; Canberra, Australia; California; and South Carolina. She currently lives with her husband in Simpsonville, South Carolina.